ARISE JOSHUA GENERATION

JOSEPH SAMUEL

DEDICATION

I want to dedicate this book to my parents, late Evangelist V.I. Samuel and late Mrs. Kunjamma Samuel, who are with the Lord. They served the Lord in His vineyard for sixty years. The faith journey of my father and the prayer life of my mother influenced me from a very young age. They were instrumental in shaping me and imparted into me true values of life. I learned from them that serving God is the greatest privilege one can have in this earth.

"My son, hear the instruction of your father, and do not forsake the law of your mother" (Proverbs 1:8)

ARISE JOSHUA GENERATION

CONTENTS

Dedication | 03

Acknowledgements | 07

Foreword | 09

Introduction | 13

Chapter 1
Arise Joshua Generation | 17

Chapter 2
The Death of Self | 19

Chapter 3
A New Dispensation | 29

Chapter 4
A New Commission | 35

Chapter 5
Possessing the Land | 39

Chapter 6
Enlarge your Territory | 45

Chapter 7
Divine Protection | 53

Chapter 8
Divine Presence | 57

Chapter 9
Joshua, Why Are You Still Waiting? | 63

Chapter 10
End Time Stock Of God | 67

Chapter 11
Joshua Generation is Ready! | 71

ACKNOWLEDGEMENTS

First, I want to thank my Lord Jesus for everything and for considering me worthy of His call. All I am and I have is because of my loving Savior. I want to thank my wife Elizabeth, my son Blesson, his wife Christy, my daughter Blessy and her husband Denny, who always stood by my side, which helped me in completing this book. A special thanks to my son Evangelist Blesson Joseph for his help in reviewing this book. I also want to thank my siblings for their prayers, support and encouragement to write this book.

I want to thank the men and women of God, whom God used over the years to give me prophetic words about writing books, and also the encouragement by countless friends and well-wishers.

A big thank you to Global Revival and Harvest Center (Revival Harvest Church) for supporting this work. God is touching nations through this ministry.

Last, but not the least, I want to express my special thanks to Apostle Femi Adun, and Grace House Publishing for editing and publishing this book.

FOREWORD

The life of Joshua exemplifies what God wants to do with this generation, our generation. The Joshua generation is a generation God is raising in this dispensation. God's work with Moses was very significant in that He played in the fulfillment of the promise He gave to Abraham, a rescue (deliverance) mission. However, Joshua's assignment was of greater necessity and impact (Deuteronomy 31:1-8).

Moses' generation was a sign, wonder & miracle generation, but God demanded more from Joshua's generation. It isn't comforting to observe that without Moses's miraculous acts, he did not have a strong leadership position with Israel's children. The performance of sign, wonder & miracle does not make one a Leader. Indeed, this present time's church needs to be weaned off the gospel as only presented in the building's four walls.

There is a responsibility on the church of this generation that demands sound Spiritual Leadership capacity and Character. God demanded leadership from Joshua, the same way He is demanding leadership from us. God does not only want to deliver a nation, but He ultimately wants to lead nations into His plans and purposes. While Moses's first task was to PERFORM A MIRACLE; on the other hand, Joshua's first task was not to show the mighty acts of God, but the incredible leadership ability of God.

"Then Joshua commanded the officers of the people, saying, "Pass through the camp and command the people, saying, 'Prepare provisions for yourselves, for within three days you will cross over this Jordan, to go in to possess the land which the LORD your God is giving you to possess." - (Joshua 1:10).

Many of the people who come to our churches today are after signs, wonder & miracle, which is okay, but it becomes destructive when parishioners cannot lead. Authentic leadership empowers others and releases them to fulfill God's plan. I believe that spiritual leadership is the last phase of the church's assignment because we stand in between the timeline of two-generation where sound spiritual leadership is required to bring to pass God's plan for the last days as we see with Moses and Joshua.

In Isaiah 2:3, The scriptures say that out of Zion shall come forth the law. Zion is not a physical location; it's where believers are gathered or gathering. The truth is that in our gatherings, we have raised powerful intercessors, great preachers, quality musicians, and exceptional ushers and catchers. Still, God is asking when my church will begin to raise LAWMAKERS, DECISION MAKERS, STATESMEN, COUNSEL MEN, GOVERNORS, MAYORS, AND EVEN PRESIDENTS / PRIME MINISTERS. We need men catchers, but we need nations, community, family, economy, Government, media catchers, etc.

"The scepter or leadership shall not depart from Judah, nor the ruler's staff from between his feet, until Shiloh the Messiah, the Peaceful One comes to Whom it belongs, and to Him shall be the obedience of the people." - Genesis 49:10 AMPC.

Leadership is the church's end-time assignment; it's the church's final work before Christ comes because the world has not come across the current level of leadership crises or decadence. The most destructive pandemic the world will have to deal with is immoral, ineffective, corrupt, and selfish leadership. Our family, ministry, business, cities, and nation are at the mercy of kingdom leadership that will bring real transformation, and this is what Joshua generation represents - Spiritual (Prophetic) Leadership, Servant Leadership, Apostolic Leadership, Governmental Leadership, and Family Leadership.

I am truly honored by my dear friend and brother in Christ to write the foreword to his first book – THIS BOOK. 'Arise Joshua Generation' is not just an epilogue but also a clarion call for believers and ministers of this present generation to wake up and assume our duty post. Pastor Joseph Samuel is a man of accurate prophetic insight, and this book is with a balanced, yet in a simplified approach that provides prophetic directives and instructions for kingdom advancement. If you sense you belong to the rising army of the Lord and want to know how to position yourself, then you have the right tool in your hand.

Brother Joseph, congratulations, and thank you for yielding to the Lord. I do not doubt that this divine download will challenge a higher standard in the body of Christ and draw souls to our Lord, Jesus Christ. Amen!

Apostle Femi Adun
President, Eagle World Outreach

INTRODUCTION

The vision of Joshua generation birthed in me in the year 2000. On the day of my ordination as a Pastor, I was literally on the floor in my home weeping before the Lord. I was wrestling with the Lord as I did not want to be a Pastor. I knew I was called to proclaim the good news as I have been doing it in the streets and places wherever the Lord opened the door for me. I was involved in different facets of the ministry of the church - Sunday School, Youth Ministry, Prayer Meetings and Intercessory groups, but I did not want to Pastor a Church. The Lord told me it was Him doing it and I had to accept it. On that day, the Lord spoke to me from Joshua Chapter 1 "You are part of a Joshua Generation. You are called to lead Joshua Generation and prepare Joshua Generation".

The Lord spoke to me through many servants of God for almost twenty years that I should write a book. I did not want to write a book. First of all, it is not my area of strength. Secondly, there are hundreds and hundreds of scholarly books written by mighty men and women of God. I did not want to add one more from me. A few years ago, Holy Spirit spoke to me through a prophet "Over the years I have been speaking to you directly and through my servants that you should write books and you have been ignoring it; it is not a suggestion; it is my command." I asked the Lord His forgiveness for my disobedience.

I started writing this book, but I left it undone. A few months ago the Lord reminded me again during my prayer "I cannot release what I have in store for you until you are in complete obedience to me and finish the task you started." This has prompted me to finish the task and that is why you are getting this book in your hand.

The intent of writing this book is not to bring a scholarly or a doctrinal subject, but to convey what the Holy Spirit instilled in my heart on the subject over the years. I have been preaching on Joshua Generation partially in many places. Now I am thrilled to finally have it in print.

In this book, I will endeavor to bring the truth out. We do not build the Kingdom of God. Holy Spirit does. Jesus said, "I will build My church, and the gates of Hades shall not prevail against it". God does not build our church or kingdom; He builds His church – His Kingdom. Nevertheless, He uses us – He is the Picture, we are the frame; He is the Source, we are the vessel. It pleased the

Heavenly Father to involve us to show forth His Glory! Hallelujah! His Glory is revealed when He is visible; He is visible when we become invisible. This demands a total surrender from us. When we surrender ourselves fully to the Lord, we become part of the Joshua Generation. Joshua Generation does not just hear the promise, does not just see the promise, they occupy the promise.

It is my prayer that as we read this book, the Holy Spirit will open our eyes of understanding to know His plans for our life and that we totally surrender to Him, thereby we become part of Joshua Generation to occupy the promises of the Lord.

Welcome to the era of Joshua Generation!

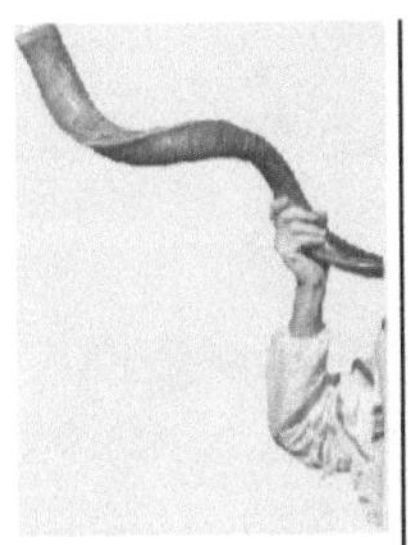

CHAPTER 1

ARISE JOSHUA GENERATION

After the death of Moses the servant of the Lord, it came to pass that the Lord spoke to Joshua the son of Nun, Moses' assistant, saying: "Moses My servant is dead. Now therefore, arise, go over this Jordan, you and all this people, to the land which I am giving to them—the children of Israel. Every place that the sole of your foot will tread upon I have given you, as I said to Moses. From the wilderness and this Lebanon as far as the great river, the River Euphrates, all the land of the Hittites, and to the Great Sea toward the going down of the sun, shall be your territory. No man shall be able to stand before you all the days of your life; as I was with Moses, so I will be with you. I will not leave you nor forsake you. Be strong and of good courage, for to this people you shall divide as an inheritance the land which I swore to their fathers to give them. Joshua 1: 1-6

Yes indeed, we are the New Generation!

Generally, when we talk about Joshua generation, a group of young people come to our mind. No doubt, it refers to a group of young people. But, as I understand, Joshua and Caleb in today's terms are senior citizens. So, it does not refer to a physical age, but to a generation who knows their position and possession in Jesus Christ. In other words, a generation whose mind is renewed knowing that they are heavenly citizens, though still living in the earth, they are seated with Christ in the heavenly places; knowing their Christ-given authority and the power of the Holy Spirit. Though their outward man may weary yet the inner man is strengthened day by day, from strength to strength, from grace to grace, faith to faith and glory to glory.

They draw their strength from the Lord himself; as we read in Isaiah 40:30-31 "Even the youths shall faint and be weary, And the young men shall utterly fall, But those who wait on the Lord Shall renew their strength; They shall mount up with wings like eagles, They shall run and not be weary, They shall walk and not faint." Joshua generation is young in vision and young in their action. They understand the season of the Lord. They understand the calling and purpose.

CHAPTER 2

THE DEATH
OF SELF

God spoke after the death of Moses. Old is gone, something new started.

Moses' generation was a powerful generation. The Lord brought Israel out of Egypt with a mighty hand and an outstretched arm, with great terror and with signs and wonders. The leadership of Moses is incomparable. In Acts 7:22, we read Moses was taught all the wisdom of the Egyptians, and he was powerful in both speech and action. God appeared to him in the bush as a fire. Moses spoke to God face to face. They witnessed how the mighty hand delivered them from the power of Pharaoh.

In 1 Corinthians 10, we read they were all under the cloud and that they all passed through the sea. They were all baptized into Moses in the cloud and in the sea. They all ate the same spiritual food and drank the same spiritual drink, for they drank from the spiritual rock that accompanied them, and the rock was Christ. Moses himself testified *"There is no one like the God of Jeshurun, Who rides the heavens to help you, And in His excellency on the clouds.."* (Deut. 33:26).

Nevertheless, God was not pleased with most of them, their bodies were scattered in the wilderness. Even Moses himself could not enter the promised land; he could only see it. The reason they could not enter is mentioned in 1 Corinthians 10. Among them, only Joshua and Caleb entered the promised land; why? Because they were different.

God waited until Moses' generation was over. This in no way is to minimize the greatness of Moses or his leadership. Though he did not enter into the physical promised land, he is the only one in the history of mankind whose burial was conducted by the Almighty God Himself. He is one of the two who appeared on the Mount of Transfiguration. There are two songs being sung in eternity - the song of the Lamb of God and the song of Moses. They sing the song of Moses, the servant of God, and the song of the Lamb, saying: *"Great and marvelous are Your works, Lord God Almighty! Just and true are Your ways, O King of the saints!"* (Revelation 15:3). The message I would like to emphasize here is not about the Moses outside us; but the Moses inside of us.

This is the secret. Before the foundations of the world, the Lord has chosen us in Him. Yes indeed, before we were formed in our mother's womb, God has already chosen us.

Before we were formed, we were hidden in the Father's heart - our design, our purpose, our destiny. *"For You formed my inward parts; You covered me in my mother's womb"* (Psalms 139:13). Genesis 1:26-28 *"Then God said, "Let Us make man in Our image, according to Our likeness; let them have dominion over the fish of the sea, over the birds of the air, and over the cattle, over all the earth and over every creeping thing that creeps on the earth." So God created man in His own image; in the image of God He created him; male and female He created them. Then God blessed them, and God said to them, "Be fruitful and multiply; fill the earth and subdue it; have dominion over the fish of the sea, over the birds of the air, and over every living thing that moves on the earth." But when we read Genesis 2:7 "And the Lord God formed man of the dust of the ground, and breathed into his nostrils the breath of life; and man became a living being." We call it outer man and inner man. The outer man is formed from the dust of the ground while the inner man is created in the image and likeness of God."*

Therefore, I am not talking about the leader Moses; I am talking about us; we have a Moses in us and also, we have a Joshua in us. The Moses in us represents our old man; the first Adam, the fallen one. The Joshua in us represents the last Adam, the new man Christ in us. The old has to die in order for the new to operate. The flesh has to die before the Holy Spirit can manifest in our lives.

This experience has to take place in each one of us. Sometimes, the little things we hold, or we consider may be more important for God. We will see this truth in the life of Prophet Isaiah, who experienced a total transformation when he encountered a divine revelation. Because of this revelation, Isaiah no longer remained ordinary but from that moment he emerged as a prophet of God. Let's examine this in the scriptures below.

Isaiah 6:1-9 *"In the year that King Uzziah died, I saw the Lord sitting on a throne, high and lifted up, and the train of His robe filled the temple. Above it stood seraphim; each one had six wings: with two he covered his face, with two he covered his feet, and with two he flew. And one cried to another and said: "Holy, holy, holy is the Lord of hosts; The whole earth is full of His glory!" And the posts of the door were shaken by the voice of him who cried out, and the house was filled with smoke. So I said: "Woe is me, for I am undone! Because I am a man of unclean lips, And I dwell in the midst of a people of unclean lips; For my eyes have seen the King, The Lord of hosts." Then one of the seraphim flew to me, having in his hand a live coal which he had taken with the tongs from the altar. And he touched my mouth with it, and said: "Behold, this has touched your lips; Your iniquity is taken away, And your sin purged." Also I heard the voice of the Lord, saying: "Whom shall I send, And who will go for Us?" Then I said, "Here am I! Send me." And He said, "Go, and tell this people: 'Keep on hearing, but do not understand; Keep on seeing, but do not perceive.'*

We can read about the reign of King Uzziah in 2 Chronicles 26 and 2 Kings 15:1-7 (Uzziah is called Azariah here). King Uzziah of Judah was a distinguished king. He became a king at the age of 16 and he reigned for a long 52 years. Generally speaking, he was a good king and he did what was right in the sight of the Lord, according to all that his father Amaziah had done (2 Chr. 15:3). He sought God in the days of Zechariah, who had understanding in the visions of God; and as long as he sought the LORD, God made him prosper (2 Chr. 26:5). He was a strong king having victories over neighboring nations. His fame spread as far as the entrance of Egypt, for he strengthened himself exceedingly (2 Chr. 26:8). But we read in 2 Chronicles 26:16, "But when he was strong his heart was lifted up, to his destruction, for he transgressed against the Lord his God by entering the temple of the Lord to burn incense on the altar of incense." We know this duty was given to the priest only. Even the attempt of the priest to stop him was not successful because of the pride of the king. In response, God struck Uzziah with leprosy, and he was an isolated leper until his death.

How did the tragic death of king Uzziah affect Prophet Isaiah for God to give him a special revelation? Some suggest Isaiah and king Uzziah were related - first cousins. Even otherwise it is evident Prophet Isaiah had a good influence upon the life of king Uzziah. Let me address it as to how the Holy Spirit influenced my life with this incident.

Firstly, what a blessing and protection for a prophet to have the backing of the king. Secondly, who would replace this strong, powerful and great king to reign in Judah, to protect and prosper the nation? Therefore, it was natural that prophet Isaiah and the people of Judah were praying for healing the king so he would be on the throne again. Thirdly, this king in general was a good king doing right in the sight of God, and what is a big deal of one small slip on his part entering the temple of the LORD to burn incense on the altar? But God did not answer the prayer of the people nor the prophet.

King Uzziah was neither healed nor returned to his throne; instead he died. This not only put a question in the mind of the people and the prophet but also it became a talk (we can see it by the fire touching the tongue of the prophet) – why did not God answer our prayers – why did not God forgive this king and heal him – after all, it was a small mistake he committed (according to human standard) – who would replace this king? Why, why, why, is it not injustice?

God gave prophet Isaiah a revelation (vision) - not the people, but the prophet, because **revelation is personal**. **Revelation comes from God and not from people**. *"In the year that King Uzziah died, I saw the Lord sitting on a throne, high and lifted up, and the train of His robe filled the temple."* Isaiah the earthly king may be dead, but look up, the heavenly King is not dead; the King of kings – who appoints kings and remove kings – is still on the throne. He is still in control. He has the authority to rule forever – His kingdom and throne is forever. He is high and exalted.

Hallelujah, the King of kings and the Lord of lords is still on the throne, no matter what is taking place in the earth!

Secondly, he saw the heavenly worship. *Above it stood seraphim; each one had six wings: with two he covered his face, with two he covered his feet, and with two he flew. And one cried to another and said: "Holy, holy, holy is the Lord of hosts; The whole earth is full of His glory."*

REVELATION REVEALS THE NATURE OF GOD

Isaiah - the Lord is Holy. Holy! Holy! Holy! 'And the foundations of the thresholds trembled at the voice of him who called out, and the temple was filled with smoke.' Isaiah - not only the Lord is holy, the worship is holy. There is no shortage of smoke (incense) in heaven, the heavenly temple is full of incense - God's glory! The angelic hosts are worshipping Him always, because He alone is worthy to be worshipped. What a privilege God has given mankind to worship Him. All creation worships the Creator. *"The heavens declare the glory of God; And the firmament shows His handiwork" (Psalms 19:1).* What a privilege God has given mankind to worship Him. I thank God for the blood of Jesus that qualifies us to worship this living God. Isaiah - heaven is not short of worship (incense); offering the incense is not a small thing, it is the main thing; God does not change His nature and standard. Those who worship Him must worship Him in spirit and in truth; acknowledging His holiness.

REVELATION BRINGS TRANSFORMATION IN OUR LIFE

The revelation of heavenly worship changed Isaiah. It changed him forever. It changed his nature, his character, and even his ministry. *"Woe is me, for I am undone! Because I am a man of unclean lips, And I dwell in the midst of a people of unclean lips; For my eyes have seen the King, The Lord of hosts."* Isaiah acknowledged his fault – the tongue. Yes, what people talked; and he became a part of it. He confessed and realized he was at fault. Yes indeed, this is the beginning of the death of the man Isaiah (the old man). The old man had to die.

REVELATION IMPARTS GOD INTO OUR LIFE

The fire touched the mouth of Isaiah. This touch was very unique. *The fire was brought by one of the seraphims directly from the throne of God. "Then one of the seraphim flew to me, having in his hand a live coal which he had taken with the tongs from the altar. And he touched my mouth with it, and said: "Behold, this has touched your lips; Your iniquity is taken away, And your sin purged."* This touch of fire purified Isaiah for His call. It resembles what John the Baptist declared about Jesus *"He will baptize you with the Holy Ghost and with Fire."* On the day of Pentecost, this is what happened. Holy Spirit came down as a fire. Fire can melt us and remove those things in our life, which are contrary to our call. Gold is purified in the fire. I know the blood of Jesus washes us; cleans us;

justifies us; sanctifies us. But we still have old man's nature that only fire can remove. Then it is no longer us, but Him. We are not visible, but Jesus is visible in our life. The best is that the Fire never leaves us; He is with us, wherever we go, whatever we do! Hallelujah!

REVELATION GIVES US A COMMISSION

Fire of God comes in our life for a purpose. It comes with a commission: *Also I heard the voice of the Lord, saying: "Whom shall I send, And who will go for Us?" Then I said, "Here am I! Send me."*

I recollect a vision the Lord gave me in one of my mission trips in 2013. I was in a local flight from Sao Paulo, Brazil to Santa Catarina, Brazil. My flight was about to touch down, then the Lord showed me the vision. I saw an ocean of fire. I saw millions in that fire. They were screaming and trying to get out of it. I saw some black birds flying over them and pushing them down, so they could not get out. I asked the Lord what He wanted to communicate with me. I heard the voice of the Lord from Isaiah 6:8 "Whom shall I send, and who will go for me?" I felt the heart of God. Holy Spirit spoke to me – Jesus died for all mankind, but millions and millions are perishing and going to hell without Christ! I could not hold my tears. On the last day of the three-day convention, I shared this vision and preached from Isaiah 6. I saw many – young and old - at the altar committing their lives for full time ministry that night. Hallelujah!

> The revelation comes with a price tag! Whom shall I send, and who will go for me? Are you the one the Lord is looking for?

This touch of fire truly changed Isaiah's perspective. It changed his ministry. From Isaiah chapter 6, the ministry of Isaiah changed. It did not matter who will listen to him; or who will understand him. He just became a voice of the Lord. That is what true revelation does. We will not be men pleasers, but God pleasers. We will join with Paul and say *"For do I now persuade men, or God? Or do I seek to please men? For if I still pleased men, I would not be a bondservant of Christ"* (Galatians 1:10).

Is Moses in us dead and Joshua in us ready?

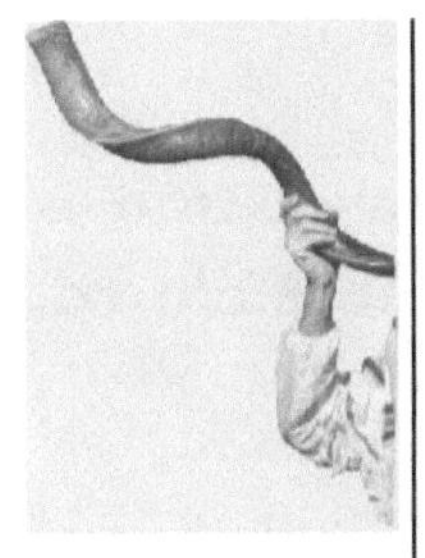

CHAPTER 3

A New Dispensation

We read in Joshua chapter 1 that after the death of Moses, God spoke to Joshua, son of Nun. Maybe it was strange to Joshua why God was repeating that Moses was dead because Joshua knew it already. Not only Joshua, all Israelites knew it. In fact, all Israelites, including Joshua, mourned for Moses for thirty days. Then, why was God repeating it to Joshua? Moses already summoned Joshua as we read in *Deuteronomy 31:7-8: "Then Moses called Joshua and said to him in the sight of all Israel, "Be strong and of good courage, for you must go with this people to the land which the Lord has sworn to their fathers to give them, and you shall cause them to inherit it. And the Lord, He is the One who goes before you. He will be with you, He will not leave you nor forsake you; do not fear nor be dismayed."* It implied there is an inherent meaning with God emphasizing it to Joshua. God knew it and Joshua also knew it. God himself did the burial service for Moses. However, when God emphasized it; there was a hidden meaning in it. God was testifying it.

It means the old season is gone; a new season is coming. God testifies it. The old chapter is closed, and God is opening a new chapter.

Even in Moses life, he had to die to himself before God could use him. Moses was the right fit as he was chosen by the Lord before he was formed in his mother's womb. He was the right man fit for the job. He was raised in Egypt. He was also trained in Egypt. In Acts 7:22 we read *"And Moses was learned in all the wisdom of the Egyptians, and was mighty in words and deeds."* However, in order for the supernatural to take place his natural ability had to die. Not only God had to testify it, he had to do it by faith. The book of Hebrews 11:23-29 describes it: *"By faith Moses, when he was born, was hidden three months by his parents, because they saw he was a beautiful child; and they were not afraid of the king's command. By faith Moses, when he became of age, refused to be called the son of Pharaoh's daughter, choosing rather to suffer affliction with the people of God than to enjoy the passing pleasures of sin, esteeming the reproach of Christ greater riches than the treasures in Egypt; for he looked to the reward. By faith he forsook Egypt, not fearing the wrath of the king; for he endured as seeing Him who is invisible. By faith he kept the Passover and the sprinkling of blood, lest he who destroyed the firstborn should touch them. By faith they passed through the Red Sea as by dry land, whereas the Egyptians, attempting to do so, were drowned."*

According to Moses, he was ready after 40 years of training in the palace in Egypt, but not according to God. While

Moses was counting in ascending order from one to forty in his credentials, God started counting in descending order from forty to one. God took him to wilderness experience taking care of sheep. As every year passed by, Moses started realizing himself, that he was unfit for the job. But it was at that moment, after 40 years of training in Egypt and 40 years in the wilderness, Moses realized he was unfit for the job. Then God appeared to Moses. *"And the Angel of the Lord appeared to him in a flame of fire from the midst of a bush. So he looked, and behold, the bush was burning with fire, but the bush was not consumed"* (Exodus 3:2).

But now Moses knew it was too late. He was a zero, unfit for the job. We read in Exodus 4:10-13 *"Then Moses said to the Lord, "O my Lord, I am not eloquent, neither before nor since You have spoken to Your servant; but I am slow of speech and slow of tongue." So the Lord said to him, "Who has made man's mouth? Or who makes the mute, the deaf, the seeing, or the blind? Have not I, the Lord? Now therefore, go, and I will be with your mouth and teach you what you shall say." But he said, "O my Lord, please send by the hand of whomever else You may send."* A man well trained in Egypt - man of power in words and deeds – considered himself unfit!

When Moses considered himself unfit, God considered him fit. God promised him that I (THE GREAT I AM) am with you. It is not you; it is ME; now you are ready.

I want to personalize this message. We all have a Moses in us, and maybe it is a wonderful experience, but our God is a God of seasons! He is the same yesterday, today and forever! That means, He is God of Yesterday, God of Today, and God of Tomorrow. He has a season for Moses; He has a season for Joshua. We all have a Moses in us; the old man; the one who is more experienced; the one who is more capable; the one who is well trained; the one who wants to take glory for himself; the one who will never surrender; the one who does not want to obey the Lord in everything. Yes, he has to die.

The Joshua in us has to arise – the one who considers himself incapable; the one who waits upon the Lord; the one who can move only by God's power; the one who will totally surrender to God and confess as Jesus did at the Garden of Gethsemane "yet not my will, let thy will be done." We have to die with Him in order to resurrect with Him. Then we can Join with Paul and say *that I may know Him and the power of His resurrection, and the fellowship of His sufferings, being conformed to His death"* (Philippians 3:10).

> It is one thing to surrender; it is another thing
> for God to confirm it. We cannot bury Moses;
> God has to bury him, and God has to confirm it.
> That is called victory! Yes indeed, then the
> Joshua in us will come out!

Now Joshua in us is ready to come out.

We are now ready to experience the new life in Christ. New doors are waiting for us. The new chapter is waiting for us. In this new chapter, we will forget the pain and suffering of the old chapter. Get ready for the new chapter!

CHAPTER 4

A New Commission

Now then, you and all these people, get ready to cross the Jordan River into the Land I am about to give to them – to the Israelites.

Yes, there is a Jordan River. We cannot avoid it. But we have to overcome it. Between us and the promise, there is always a Jordan River. And the important fact is *"Jordan River is at flood stage all during harvest"* (Joshua 3:15). We have to cross it – we cannot pray it out, we cannot fast it out, we cannot run away from it. We have to buckle our belt and cross it. We cannot do it with our strength – *it is not by might, it is not by power, but by the Spirit.* Do not wait for Jordan River to wet our feet, but we step on it, not alone, with the ark (the Spirit). It may not understand us (the creation), but it understands the Spirit (the Creator); it may not understand our language, but it understands the language of the Spirit.

Many times, we wait for God to dry the Jordan River,

whereas God may be waiting on us to step in that river with His power. **That is called partnership. We are the frame and He is the picture. We are the vessels and He is the power. We are the instrument; He is the source.**

The interesting thing is when the priests carrying the Ark put their feet in the river, the water from upstream stopped flowing. It piled up in a heap, a great distance away. That means **"Jordan River said, my time is over, now I cannot flow anymore; my power is defeated."**

God has given us the authority. Not our authority but His Authority. Many times, the authority of men becomes a hindrance for His authority to work. Jesus said, all authority in Heaven and Earth is given unto Me. Therefore, you go…. Yes, it is His authority given to us, but we are the one going. I pray we are able to hear the voice of the Holy Spirit…Therefore, you go… get up and go… do not sit down with the authority… get up and go…. And do not wait, but step in that River of Jordan (that problem), it will give way.

Because of this New Authority, a shift is coming. Things that did not move before will move. In the new season, God has prepared a new table for His children. While we were weeping and crying being stuck in our situations, the Heavenly Father was preparing a table. In the night season, we all cry. But do not worry the morning is coming.

Weeping may endure for a night, but joy comes in the morning (Psalm 30:5). Can we imagine what God has placed on the table He has prepared? But the problem we encounter is, instead of seeing the dishes God has placed on the new table, we look around and see the enemies standing and we become afraid of those enemies/problems.

Psalms 23:5 *"You prepare a table before me in the presence of my enemies; You anoint my head with oil; My cup runs over."* If God has prepared a table for us, the table is for us – it has our name. Yes, the enemies may be standing there. But between the enemies and the table, God appointed His angels to guard the table for us. I like the incident in the book of Esther. While Haman (the enemy of Mordecai and Israel) was making gallows to hang Mordecai, God was preparing a table for Mordecai.

I always thought why God did not remove Haman, who wanted to destroy Israel. The answer is that God kept Haman for a season, because he was going to be an instrument to bring the right promotion for Mordecai and God wanted to bring honor to Mordecai through his mouth. If God allowed something in our life, let us not be confused; it is for our good. Something good is about to take place. Haman could not touch the table God prepared for Mordecai; rather he became an instrument to push Mordecai towards the table.

Yes indeed, a shift is coming. Things are about to

change completely. What the enemy meant for evil God will turn it for our good. The challenges will see God! Joshua Generation, Get ready to cross – Go forward!

CHAPTER 5

POSSESSING THE LAND

I will give you every place where you set your foot, as I promised Moses.

God did not forget what He had promised to Moses. It means, our promise did not die. It may look like it is dead, may be we may think it is already buried. No, no, no. It is not dead, nor is it buried. When the appointed time of the Lord comes, even if it is buried, it will come out of the grave. All promises will be fulfilled. When God is on the move, He will not allow His children to compromise, or settle for less than what God wants in their life. *"Now to Him who is able to do exceedingly abundantly above all that we ask or think, according to the power that works in us"* (Ephesians 3:20).

He is God of abundance. *"And my God shall supply all your need according to His riches in glory by Christ Jesus"* (Philippians 4:19). That is the key; all places. Hold on to that key - every place; every promise.

Why is it important for the Joshua Generation to set their foot to occupy the land? Our God is a God of covenant. God made a covenant with Abraham. Before God made a covenant with Abraham, the Lord asked Abram to see the land by faith. *"And the Lord said to Abram, after Lot had separated from him: "Lift your eyes now and look from the place where you are—northward, southward, eastward, and westward"* (Genesis 13:14). Later on, in Genesis 15, the Lord made a covenant with Abraham that his descendants would occupy the promise *"On the same day the Lord made a covenant with Abram, saying: "To your descendants I have given this land, from the river of Egypt to the great river, the River Euphrates—the Kenites, the Kenezzites, the Kadmonites, the Hittites, the Perizzites, the Rephaim, the Amorites, the Canaanites, the Girgashites, and the Jebusites" (Genesis 15:18-21).*

Joshua Generation is not a generation that hears or sees the promise, but they occupy the promise. In fact, Moses also saw the promise. What others heard and saw; we will occupy! In order to occupy, we have to step into the promise. Why? The anointing upon Joshua generation is great! The promise is wherever you set your foot, you will occupy; it means the anointing is on the feet as well. That is what Jesus promised *"He who believes in Me, as the Scripture has said, out of his heart will flow rivers of living water"* (John 7:38).

In Ezekiel 37, we read God took prophet Ezekiel to the valley of dry bones to make an army of the Lord.

"The hand of the Lord came upon me and brought me out in the Spirit of the Lord, and set me down in the midst of the valley; and it was full of bones. Then He caused me to pass by them all around, and behold, there were very many in the open valley; and indeed they were very dry. And He said to me, "Son of man, can these bones live?" So I answered, "O Lord God, You know." Again He said to me, "Prophesy to these bones, and say to them, 'O dry bones, hear the word of the Lord! Thus says the Lord God to these bones: "Surely I will cause breath to enter into you, and you shall live. I will put sinews on you and bring flesh upon you, cover you with skin and put breath in you; and you shall live. Then you shall know that I am the Lord." So I prophesied as I was commanded; and as I prophesied, there was a noise, and suddenly a rattling; and the bones came together, bone to bone. Indeed, as I looked, the sinews and the flesh came upon them, and the skin covered them over; but there was no breath in them.

Also He said to me, "Prophesy to the breath, prophesy, son of man, and say to the breath, 'Thus says the Lord God: "Come from the four winds, O breath, and breathe on these slain, that they may live." So I prophesied as He commanded me, and breath came into them, and they lived, and stood upon their feet, an exceedingly great army" (Ezekiel 37:1-10).

Though this prophecy is concerning restoration of Israel, there is a prophetic message for each one of us. The hand of the Lord (power of God – anointing) came upon the prophet, and he was led by the Spirit of God and set him down in the middle of the valley, which was full of dry bones, scattered everywhere. Before the prophet was asked to speak the word of the Lord to the dry bones and then to prophesy to the wind, the Lord caused him to walk through these dry bones – why? I do believe as the prophet was walking, the bones were touching his feet. *"How beautiful upon the mountains Are the feet of him who brings good news, Who proclaims peace, Who brings glad tidings of good things, Who proclaims salvation, Who says to Zion, "Your God reigns!" (Isaiah 52:7).*

I do believe as the bones were touching the feet of the prophet, the river of God – the power of Invisible God manifested declaring God reigns – not death – not sickness – not curse – not powers of darkness - not demons – not spirit of death, but life, abundant life flowing.

That is the difference of Joshua generation, wherever we go the life of God flows as we are the sweet fragrance of Christ *"For we are to God the fragrance of Christ among those who are being saved and among those who are perishing" (2 Corinthians 2:15).* This is what Jesus has promised us *"Behold, I give you the authority to trample on serpents and scorpions, and over all the power of the enemy, and nothing shall by any means hurt you" (Luke 10:19).*

Joshua Generation, it is our time not just to hear about the promise or see the promise but occupy the promise. Get ready to step into your promise!

ARISE JOSHUA GENERATION

CHAPTER 6

ENLARGE YOUR TERRITORY

In this new season, God has a place for us; God has a standard for us. Our limits and limitations do not matter to God. Once we understand our position and possession in Jesus Christ, we will operate in a new realm. We will even go to the enemy's camp and occupy the promises. *"Blessed be the God and Father of our Lord Jesus Christ, who has blessed us with every spiritual blessing in the heavenly places in Christ"* (Ephesians 1:3).

I remember during my time of prayer, God showed me a vision. I saw a heap of grains. God asked me to pick up as much as I needed. In my vision, I cried and told God; "look at this small hand, how much can I take; if You give me a handful from Your hand, I will be truly blessed." My hand is small, Your Hand is Mighty: *"Who has measured the waters in the hollow of His hand, Measured heaven with a span And calculated the dust of the earth in a measure? Weighed the mountains in scales And the hills in a balance?"* (Isaiah 40:12).

Yes, if He measures for us; there is no limit. That is why we should make a decision that we would rather please God than men. Psalms 16:5-6 states *"O Lord, You are the portion of my inheritance and my cup; You maintain my lot. The lines have fallen to me in pleasant places; Yes, I have a good inheritance."* When God measures, He measures according to His standard not our standard. He will measure *"from the desert to Lebanon, and from the great river, the Euphrates, all the Hittite country – to the Great Sea on the west."* That means to the East, West, South and North: from Jerusalem, to Judea, to Samaria and to the uttermost parts of the world. We will see His overflow in every area of our life – the enemy cannot steal from any area while God blesses in the other areas of our life!

"I called on the LORD in distress; The LORD answered me and set me in a broad place" (Psalms 118:5). Distress is a place of anguish, suffering, pain and sorrow. But when our eyes of understanding are opened, we will be able to see the broad place and God places us in the broad place.

We read about a man called Jabez in 1 Chronicles 4:9-10 *"Now Jabez was more honorable than his brothers, and his mother called his name Jabez, saying, "Because I bore him in pain." And Jabez called on the God of Israel saying, "Oh, that You would bless me indeed, and enlarge my territory, that Your hand would be with me, and that You would keep me from evil, that I may not cause pain!"* So God granted him what he requested.

While 1 Chronicles chapters 1 to 8 mention the genealogy of the people, Jabez is mentioned from an unused root probably meaning to grieve; sorrowful. Nevertheless, Jabez has taken two verses in the bible. Though his own mother named him Jabez - means to grieve and sorrowful - we read that Jabez was more honorable than his brothers. What happened? How did he became more honorable? The answer is simple. One Prayer. Oh Yes! One prayer changed him. The importance is to whom he prayed. He called on the God of Israel. What is the significance of his prayer to the God of Israel in particular? Jabez got a revelation who this God is. He is God of Israel. Who is Israel? Though Israel represents a nation, first the name was given to an individual. We can find it in Genesis 32: 22-31 *And he arose that night and took his two wives, his two female servants, and his eleven sons, and crossed over the ford of Jabbok. He took them, sent them over the brook, and sent over what he had. Then Jacob was left alone; and a Man wrestled with him until the breaking of day. Now when He saw that He did not prevail against him, He touched the socket of his hip; and the socket of Jacob's hip was out of joint as He wrestled with him. And He said, "Let Me go, for the day breaks." But he said, "I will not let You go unless You bless me!" So He said to him, "What is your name?" He said, "Jacob." And He said, "Your name shall no longer be called Jacob, but Israel; for you have struggled with God and with men, and have prevailed." Then Jacob asked, saying, "Tell me Your name, I pray." And He said, "Why is it that you ask about My name?" And He blessed him there. So Jacob called the name of the place Peniel: "For*

I have seen God face to face, and my life is preserved." Just as he crossed over Penuel the sun rose on him, and he limped on his hip."

In this wresting, God asked Jacob what his name was. God knows his name very well. But God wanted him to admit it. What does Jacob mean?

In Genesis 27:36 And Esau said, *"Is he not rightly named Jacob? For he has supplanted me these two times. He took away my birthright, and now look, he has taken away my blessing!" And he said, "Have you not reserved a blessing for me?"* The meaning of his name is Supplanter or Deceitful - One Who Takes the Heel. In other words, God was telling him you could deceive your brother or even your father, but it would not work with me. The question is how could he wrestle with God? Why did God Almighty ask the permission of a mere man formed out of the dust to let him go? First of all, God Almighty came down there so that Jacob could hold him. But how could he hold him?

In Hosea 12: 3-4 *He took his brother by the heel in the womb, And in his strength he struggled with God. Yes, he struggled with the Angel and prevailed; He wept, and sought favor from Him. He found Him in Bethel, And there He spoke to us".* **It was not with the physical strength Jacob held God, but power of his tears. Yes, tears are powerful. God cannot move when His children are in His presence with tears. They are holding God.** God told Jacob, because of your tears, I am going to change your name.

You are no longer Jacob, but Israel - one that struggled with the divine angel; one who has prevailed with God; a man that saw God – the one who has the authority to rule, means a prince. Not only did God change His name, but God also changed His destiny to become a nation - nation of Israel.

Jabez caught this revelation. God who could change his name and destiny. He prayed to God of Israel. In other words, Jabez said, Lord, I know who you are. You are God of Israel. You are my God also. As you blessed Jacob, bless me also, as you increased his territory enlarge my territory as well, as you kept him from all evil, keep me also from evil so that my destiny is changed. God granted him what he requested. Hallelujah! God has no favoritism. He is not only God of Israel (Jacob) and Jabez but also our God

> When God manifests between our past and future, our destiny changes!

The secret is we should see things as God sees it. God called Abraham to become Father of Nations. We read the promise given to him in Genesis 12. Yet, Abraham had to align himself to the increase God declared in his life. We read in Genesis 15:1-6 *"After these things the word of the Lord came to Abram in a vision, saying, "Do not be afraid, Abram. I am your shield, your exceedingly great reward." But Abram said, "Lord God, what will You give me, seeing I go childless, and the heir of my house is Eliezer of Damascus?" Then Abram said, "Look, You have given me no offspring; indeed one born in my house is my heir!" And behold, the word of the Lord came to him, saying, "This one shall not be your heir, but one who will come from your own body shall be your heir." Then He brought him outside and said, "Look now toward heaven, and count the stars if you are able to number them." And He said to him, "So shall your descendants be." And he believed in the Lord, and He accounted it to him for righteousness.*

ABRAHAM'S VISION CHANGED

God took him out of the box for Abraham to see the plan of God. Look up, your children will be like stars in the sky. In Genesis 22:17, *"blessing I will bless you, and multiplying I will multiply your descendants as the stars of the heaven and as the sand which is on the seashore; and your descendants shall possess the gate of their enemies."* **In other words, whether Abraham looked up or looked down, he started seeing the promise of God – increase.**

HIS NAME CHANGED

We read in Genesis 17: 5 *"No longer shall your name be called Abram, but your name shall be Abraham; for I have made you a father of many nations."* From Abram – *exalted father, God changed his name to Abraham – father of many nations.* Why did God change his name? In my view, God changed his name, so he would speak the promise of God and he would hear the promise of God. Next day, when Abraham got out of his house, people called him Abram, he said No, I am Abraham. He started saying the promise; the following day people called him Abraham, he started hearing the promise of God. God changed the name of Sarai also. Instead of Sarai, God changed her name to Sarah, means mother of nations, as kings of people shall be of her (Genesis 17:15-16).

This is the secret. Unless we see like God sees, the increase does not take place in our life. We need to associate ourselves with people of same stream who believe in increase. Chicken and Eagle cannot walk together. **We should see the promise, hear the promise and speak the promise. Once we are aligned with the promise of God, increase begins.**

52

CHAPTER 7

DIVINE PROTECTION

In this new season, there is a divine protection. Even the hairs of our head are numbered. Until the purpose is fulfilled, the enemy cannot touch us. It is not just for a season, but all the days of our life. The Lord promised us *"I will be with you until the end."*

The enemy may form weapons against us, and it may look like he is going to shoot those weapons, and he may even shoot the weapons, but it will not prosper. *"No weapon formed against you shall prosper, And every tongue which rises against you in judgment You shall condemn. This is the heritage of the servants of the Lord, And their righteousness is from Me, Says the Lord"* (Isaiah 54:17).

While the enemy may laugh at us and show us His weapons, if our eyes are opened we will see heavenly troops standing to protect us. We read a wonderful testimony in 2 Kings Chapter 6 how God protects His own. 2 King 6: 8-18 *"Now the king of Syria was making war against Israel; and he consulted with his servants, saying, "My camp will be in such and such a place." And the man of God sent to the king of Israel, saying, "Beware that you do not pass this place, for the Syrians are coming down there." Then the king of Israel sent someone to the place of which the man of God had told him. Thus he warned him, and he was watchful there, not just once or twice. Therefore the heart of the king of Syria was greatly troubled by this thing; and he called his servants and said to them, "Will you not show me which of us is for the king of Israel?" And one of his servants said, "None, my lord, O king; but Elisha, the prophet who is in Israel, tells the king of Israel the words that you speak in your bedroom." So he said, "Go and see where he is, that I may send and get him." And it was told him, saying, "Surely he is in Dothan." Therefore he sent horses and chariots and a great army there, and they came by night and surrounded the city. And when the servant of the man of God arose early and went out, there was an army, surrounding the city with horses and chariots. And his servant said to him, "Alas, my master! What shall we do?" So he answered, "Do not fear, for those who are with us are more than those who are with them." And Elisha prayed, and said, "Lord, I pray, open his eyes that he may see." Then the Lord opened the eyes of the young man, and he saw. And behold, the mountain was full of horses and chariots of fire all around Elisha. So when the Syrians came down to him, Elisha prayed to the Lord, and said, "Strike this people, I pray, with blindness." And He struck them with blindness according to the word of Elisha.*

It may look like we are alone in certain situations, but we are not. When the time comes, God will manifest Himself.

The invisible will become visible. That is why, we do not have to fight it – the battle belongs to the Lord.

The Lord is not walking with us side by side. He is in front of us. He is the captain of the Army. Let us move forward under His divine protection, as He will hide us under his wings. May Psalm 91 be written deep inside of our hearts and let it minister to us when the enemy tries to bring fear into our life.

Psalm 91:1-8

He who dwells in the secret place of the Most High Shall abide under the shadow of the Almighty. I will say of the Lord, "He is my refuge and my fortress; My God, in Him I will trust." Surely He shall deliver you from the snare of the fowler And from the perilous pestilence. He shall cover you with His feathers, And under His wings you shall take refuge; His truth shall be your shield and buckler. You shall not be afraid of the terror by night, Nor of the arrow that flies by day, Nor of the pestilence that walks in darkness, Nor of the destruction that lays waste at noonday. A thousand may fall at your side, And ten thousand at your right hand; But it shall not come near you. Only with your eyes shall you look, And see the reward of the wicked."

Yes indeed, we are under Divine Protection!

CHAPTER 8

DIVINE PRESENCE

"As I was with Moses, so I will be with you; I will never leave you nor forsake you".

This is the secret; this is the success; this is the confidence – the Lord is with us. God says "yes, I did not fail Moses, I was with him. When people questioned him, I was with him. When he faced Pharaoh, I was with him. When he was before Red Sea, I was with him. When he stood by the rock for the water, I was with him. When he waited for the manna, I was with him; yes indeed, I was with him always. Even when he died on that mountain, I was with him. Even I buried him with my own hand."

God was assuring Joshua, referring back to His integrity - how He was with Moses. "Joshua, you are not alone in this mission. The Lord is with you". Of course, close to two million people were there with Joshua. God did not say, Joshua my people are with you. God said, "I am and will be with you." What a wonderful experience to have the Creator with us. How blessed we are when the Source of blessing is with us!

God said, *"I will not leave you; nor forsake you."* The Lord repeated what Moses mentioned to Joshua while commissioning him. *"Be strong and of good courage, do not fear nor be afraid of them; for the Lord your God, He is the One who goes with you. He will not leave you nor forsake you." (Deut.31:6)* People may come and go. They may leave. But God is with us forever. This is not only a journey for this lifetime but even through eternity. That also means, He deserves first place in our life - in everything, in every decision.

Sometimes, we might doubt if God was really with Moses. Yes, he was. Even when Moses failed God, God did not fail Moses. Yes, Moses had to pay a price for his failure. He could not enter the physical promised land. *"And he said to them: "I am one hundred and twenty years old today. I can no longer go out and come in. Also the Lord has said to me, 'You shall not cross over this Jordan" (Deut.31:2).* Essentially, at Meribah as we read in Numbers 20, when Israel complained and cried out for water, Moses misrepresented God by angrily striking the rock twice, instead of just speaking to the rock as God commanded him. It may look like a harsh punishment. Moses marred a beautiful picture of Jesus' redemptive work through the rock that provided water in the wilderness. It is clear in 1 Corinthians 4; the life-giving water came out of Jesus. By Moses striking the rock twice, he misrepresented it, as Jesus will not become a sacrifice again. He became a sacrifice once for all. God did not take it lightly. This gives us warning on how seriously we should handle Godly things. Nevertheless, God did not leave him. Why, this was the earnest desire of Moses; in fact, the only desire of Moses – the presence of God.

> Exodus 33:12-17 *Then Moses said to the Lord, "See, You say to me, 'Bring up this people.' But You have not let me know whom You will send with me. Yet You have said, 'I know you by name, and you have also found grace in My sight.' Now therefore, I pray, if I have found grace in Your sight, show me now Your way, that I may know You and that I may find grace in Your sight. And consider that this nation is Your people." And He said, "My Presence will go with you, and I will give you rest." Then he said to Him, "If Your Presence does not go with us, do not bring us up from here. For how then will it be known that Your people and I have found grace in Your sight, except You go with us? So we shall be separate, Your people and I, from all the people who are upon the face of the earth." So the Lord said to Moses, "I will also do this thing that you have spoken; for you have found grace in My sight, and I know you by name."*

The question of Moses was whom God would send with him. Was he alone? Was he lonely? He was surrounded by multitude – leaders, Joshua, Caleb; we could keep on counting even thousands…. Why was Moses asking this question?

The eye of Moses *was fixed on God. "By faith he forsook Egypt, not fearing the wrath of the king; for he endured as seeing Him who is invisible" (Hebrews 11:27).* Moses knew it. It was the secret of his life. He was not after anything else, but God Himself. That was what led him to do what he did. God promised him. *"Behold, I send an Angel before you to keep you in the way and to bring you into the place which I have prepared. Beware of Him and obey His voice; do not provoke Him, for He will not pardon your transgressions; for My name is in Him" (Exodus 23:20).* This was the strength of Moses, the Angel who had God's name in Him (the second person of the Trinity) would be with Moses every step of the way!

Things changed when people sinned against God. Exodus 33:1-3 we read, *"Then the Lord said to Moses, "Depart and go up from here, you and the people whom you have brought out of the land of Egypt, to the land of which I swore to Abraham, Isaac, and Jacob, saying, 'To your descendants I will give it.' And I will send My Angel before you, and I will drive out the Canaanite and the Amorite and the Hittite and the Perizzite and the Hivite and the Jebusite. Go up to a land flowing with milk and honey; for I will not go up in your midst, lest I consume you on the way, for you are a stiff-necked people."* Instead of calling God's own people, God now transferred the ownership to Moses saying, *"you and the people you have brought".* God was not willing to walk with them anymore. Nevertheless, God was not able to go back with the covenant God made with Abraham. God said He would send an angel to go before them.

Moses was pleading with God to consider this nation as God's people. What made them special was God Himself! If His presence did not go with them, Moses was not ready to move further. For him, it was not about the promise; it was about the Promiser. Finally, God agreed - yes Moses, My Presence will go with you. His Presence is better and greater than anything else. Nothing can substitute it. Even at the burial ground, God was with Moses. Yes indeed; we cannot do anything without Him. He is the Author and Finisher of our Faith.

God promised Joshua - as I was with Moses, I will be with you – all the way – until the end!

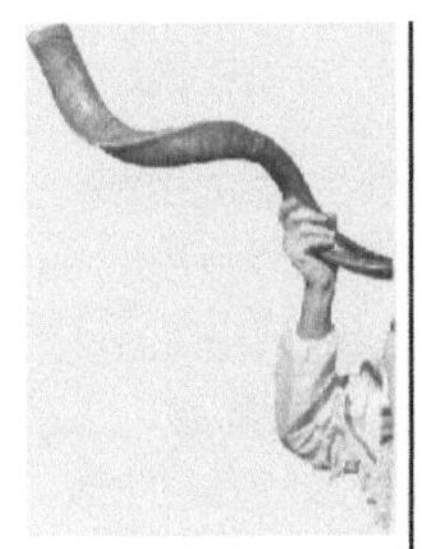

Joshua, Why Are You Still Waiting?

While all these promises are so wonderful, Joshua may have some questions in his mind. God, these promises are so wonderful. I know Moses. I know his leadership. I do not fit in his shoes. Now is the real time of warfare. How can I accomplish this assignment? You are not giving me the tools you gave to Moses.

Firstly, when you appeared to Moses, you gave him a staff (authority). Now, you are not giving me any staff. What shall I do when I am faced with challenges?

God's answer is: I know Joshua; I am not giving you any staff. In fact, it was that staff I gave to Moses that the enemy used against him. Instead of commanding the rock, out of anger, he hit the rock. That kept him away from entering into the promised land. **Therefore, I am not giving you any staff. You will be my staff. You are my tool. And what is in My hand, nobody can take away from Me!"**

AUTHORITY OF JESUS

Joshua generation, you are hidden in the hand of the Lord. He has given us the authority. A Name that is above every other name!

> *Therefore God also has highly exalted Him and given Him the name which is above every name, that at the name of Jesus every knee should bow, of those in heaven, and of those on earth, and of those under the earth, and that every tongue should confess that Jesus Christ is Lord, to the glory of God the Father* (Philippians 2:9-11)."

This Name will not fail us. In His Name, the enemy trembles. In His Name, every other name - whether in heaven, in earth or under the earth trembles; whether it be the name of demons, sickness, poverty, and so on. While we are in the hand of God, the authority is in our tongue, not in our hands. We are the mouthpiece of God.

Secondly, when you appeared to Moses in the mountain, you appeared to him in fire. "Exodus 3:1-2 *Now Moses was tending the flock of Jethro his father-in-law, the priest of Midian. And he led the flock to the back of the desert, and came to Horeb, the mountain of God. And the Angel of the Lord appeared to him in a flame of fire from the midst of a bush. So he looked, and behold, the bush was burning with fire, but the bush was not consumed."*

Joshua may say, God I do not see any fire. You appeared to Moses in the mountain as a fire. In this new season, I do not see anything tangible now. God's answer to Joshua may be

'Yes, I appeared to Moses on the mountain as a fire.' The fire was in the mountain.

Nevertheless Joshua, I am going to put this fire on you. The fire is with you. So, wherever you go, the fire is with you – when you face Jordan river; the fire is with you; when you face Jericho wall; the fire is with you; when you are in war; the fire is with you. Not only is this fire with you; it is on you; it is in you. **It is invisible now; but it becomes visible when situation arises.**

FIRE OF GOD

Yes, this fire came upon 120 on the day of Pentecost.

> *"When the Day of Pentecost had fully come, they were all with one accord in one place. And suddenly there came a sound from heaven, as of a rushing mighty wind, and it filled the whole house where they were sitting. Then there appeared to them divided tongues, as of fire, and one sat upon each of them. And they were all filled with the Holy Spirit and began to speak with other tongues, as the Spirit gave them utterance"* (Acts 2:1-4).

Wherever they went, the fire was with them: in the streets; in the marketplace; in the synagogues; when they stood before authorities; when they stood before the court; when they were in the jail. Yes, the sick were healed; demon possessed were set free; thousands were added to the kingdom of God and the kingdom of God expanded; churches were planted. The fire did not leave them; many of them became martyrs for Jesus, because the fire was with them.

They were strengthened when they were weak; they were encouraged when they were discouraged; they were empowered when they were challenged. Yes, we need this fire.

When you are alone, the fire is with you; when you are with your family, the fire is with you; when you are at work, the fire is with you; when you are in your business, the fire is with you; when you are in the pulpit, the fire is with you; when you are in the ministry, the fire is with you; when you are in the street, the fire is with you; when you are in the market, the fire is with you. The fire never leaves you! He is with you until the end! The fire will take you when Jesus appears in His glory for you to join Him. Not only is the fire with you, the fire is in you and the fire is on you! Hallelujah. **We are the end time stock of God!**

CHAPTER 10

END TIME STOCK OF GOD

We all know very well there is not much time left, as the coming of the Lord is very near. Not only do we know, but the enemy knows it as well. We are in a warfare. The devil is using all his weapons against the church as he knows his time is short. We should be aware of it and be vigilant. *1 Peter 5:8 "Be sober, be vigilant; because your adversary the devil walks about like a roaring lion, seeking whom he may devour."*

We are not an accident. We are the mystery hidden in the Father's heart. Father God has chosen us in Christ Jesus before the foundations of the world. In His time, He allowed us to come to this world. As the Lord spoke to Jeremiah, the Lord knew us before we were formed in our mother's womb; He has already sanctified us; He has already ordained us for His purpose. Not only the Lord knew us; He knew our name as well; in other words, we are not a duplicate, we are the original design of God.

Isaiah 49:1-2 *Listen, O coastlands, to Me, And take heed, you peoples from afar! The Lord has called Me from the womb; From the matrix of My mother He has made mention of My name. And He has made My mouth like a sharp sword; In the shadow of His hand He has hidden Me, And made Me a polished shaft; In His quiver He has hidden Me."*

There is life and death in our tongue. The Lord has anointed our tongue; as He touched the tongue of Jeremiah, He touched our tongue to speak life to a dead situation. Our tongue is like a sharp sword; it can cut down what the enemy has planted and build the kingdom of God.

The Lord has been protecting us from the fiery darts of the enemy. Because of our call and purpose, we are in the hit list of the enemy. While we may be in the hit list of the enemy, we are safe, as we are in the priority list of God's protection. As we read in Psalm 91, we are dwelling in the shelter of the Most High. We remain secure and rest in the shadow of the Almighty (whose power no enemy can withstand). The Lord is our refuge and our fortress. We put our full trust in our God. He will save us from the trap of the fowler and from the deadly pestilence. He covers us and completely protects us.

In a war, no country will use its most powerful weapon in the beginning; they keep the best for last. They will always hide it so the enemy will never know it. If the enemy knows, they will make antidote. **We are the end-time stock of God and the Lord has been hiding us.**

"Your arrows are sharp in the heart of the King's enemies; The peoples fall under You (Psalms 45:5)" .

The Lord never misses the target. He called us, anointed us, and was hiding us. You have been hiding for long. Enough of your invisibility. **Get ready, get ready, get ready arrows, the Hand of the Lord is about to bring the hidden arrows to light!**

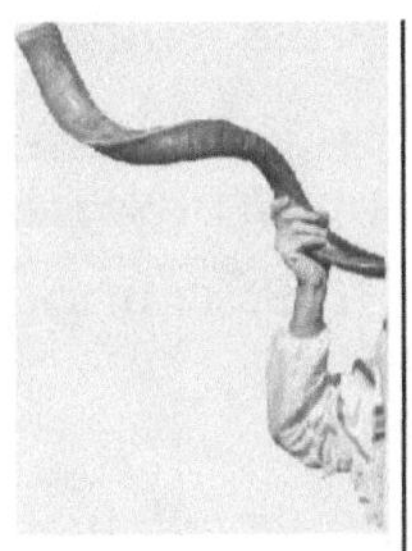

CHAPTER 11

JOSHUA GENERATION IS READY!

I would like to personalize this Chapter. As we know, as Christians, we have three enemies to deal with. Satan, the world and self.

I overcome the enemy because I know the Greater One is in me than the one in the world.

"You are of God, little children, and have overcome them, because He who is in you is greater than he who is in the world" (1 John 4:4).

By faith in the Lord I overcome the world.

"For whatever is born of God overcomes the world. And this is the victory that has overcome the world - our faith" (1 John 5:4).

The real struggle is the self (the enemy in me), who does not surrender completely to the will of God. He wants to be visible rather than reflecting Christ. In other words, I am mine own enemy to fulfill God given purpose. I realized this truth. Until I die to myself, Christ cannot manifest through me. This is what Jesus said.

> *"Most assuredly, I say to you, unless a grain of wheat falls into the ground and dies, it remains alone; but if it dies, it produces much grain "*(John 12:24).

THIS IS THE REALITY – THE SECRET

During my ministry of twenty years, along with Pastoring the church, I have been traveling to many nations conducting gospel crusades, conventions, conferences, and revival meetings. I remember in many crusades I preached from Luke 5 about Peter's catch of the fishes on a subject 'Launch the nets into deep'. In many conferences, I spoke on David's anointing. So, I knew the name of Peter well and how God used his life. I knew the name of David well and how God anointed him to be the king and how he defeated Goliath with a stone, because of the anointing upon his life.

DAVID OR THE STONES OF DAVID; PETER OR NETS OF PETER?

The year 2010 was a life changing time for me. I was on a mission trip to India. When I was ministering in Bangalore, one young Pastor, who was 25 years old came all the way from my native State to attend my meeting (this involves a train or bus travel of more than 12 hours). Let me give a little background about this young Pastor, whom God used to change my perspective about ministry.

This young Pastor knew our family very well; he was an intercessor for all of us. His father was a Pastor. In his childhood, his father went to be with the Lord. The widowed mother with great difficulty raised her son (this young Pastor) and her daughter, providing food, shelter and education. She had hoped that her son when he grew up would provide for her and his sister. With all the financial constraints, the son was able to get a graduate degree in Business Administration (MBA). In India, with an MBA one can get a lucrative job. As soon as he graduated, God called him into ministry. He shared the dealing of God and his call with the mother. With tears, the mother encouraged her son to accept the call of God. God used his life very powerfully. He did not establish a church – rather he visited many houses and led many to Christ. He was a man of prayer, a great intercessor, a prophet, and numerous lives were transformed through him. He was not famous in the list of people. He was not after name or fame. He was not looking for stages. His heart was for God's kingdom, and to bring people to the Lord.

When I went to my sister's house in my native State, this young Pastor along with his sister's husband visited me. As we were talking, the Spirit of the Lord came upon me. Immediately, I started talking to myself, which the Pastor and his brother-in-law could hear. **The Spirit of the Lord asked "you know the name of Peter, but do you know the name of the nets Peter used? You know the**

name of David, but do you know the name of the stones David used? For the end time ministry, I am not looking for Peter, but the nets he used; I am not looking for David, but the stones he used. I did not fully comprehend the dealing of the Lord then.

One year later, I got a call from my sister in India. She gave me the shocking news that this 26 years young Pastor went to be with the Lord. I could not accept it. I asked the Lord, why? Why will you call home a faithful servant at a young age? The Holy Spirit reminded me of what He spoke to me when I met with him a year ago. The Lord said 'he was my net; he was my stone; people did not know him. But when we all will appear before the judgment seat of Christ, he will be revealed'.

This truly changed me. I decided I do not want to be Peter, but I want to be a net in the Lord's hand to bring the harvest to the kingdom of God. I do not want to be David, but I want to be that stone that brings down Goliath. This changed my perspective. This changed my ministry.

I want you to ask yourself this question? Are you Peter, or the net he used? Are you David, or the stone he used? In other words, are you visible or God is visible in you?

What is true ministry? True ministry is invisible God and visible man coming together for the purpose of God! That is called ministry. When the visible becomes invisible, the invisible becomes visible.

These nets are everywhere; these stones are everywhere – in all parts of the world. They are invisible. But, they have the Authority of the Lord and the Power of the Holy Spirit. They are part of the end time revival, as they carry the seed of revival in them. They will bring the end time harvest to the kingdom of God. They are the ones God uses to build His kingdom. They will occupy the promised land. They are ready for the coming of the Lord! They are called Joshua Generation!

Arise Joshua Generation! Get ready, it is your season!

GLOBAL REVIVAL AND HARVEST CENTER

Revival Harvest Church

GlobalRevivalHarvest

globalrevivalharvest

globalrevivalharvest.org

contact@globalrevivalharvest.org

+1 231-742-8326